Friendship
NOTES

9 8 7 6 5 4 3
Digit on the right indicates the number of this printing.

ISBN 1-56138-482-8

Cover design by Toby Schmidt
Interior design by Christian Benton
Cover and interior illustrations by Valerie Coursen
Typography by Deborah Lugar
Printed in China

This book may be ordered by mail from the publisher.
Please add $1.00 for postage and handling.
But try your bookstore first!

Running Press Book Publishers
125 South Twenty-second Street
Philadelphia, PA 19103-4399

Friendship

NOTES

RUNNING PRESS
PHILADELPHIA • LONDON

. . . there is something irreducibly
mysterious about the genesis
of friendships.

Christine Leefeldt, b. 1941
American writer

Friendship is neither a formality nor a mode:
it is rather a life.

Never refuse any advance of
friendship, for if nine out of ten
bring you nothing, one alone may
repay you.

Claudine Alexandrine Tencin (1685–1749)
French writer

An acquaintance that begins with a compliment is sure to develop into a real friendship. It starts in the right manner.

Oscar Wilde (1854–1900)
Irish writer

We want but two or three friends, but these we cannot do without,

and they serve us in every thought we think.

RALPH WALDO EMERSON (1803–1882)
AMERICAN ESSAYIST AND POET

Wherever you are
it is your
own friends
who make
your world.

William James (1842–1910)
American psychologist and philosopher

In reality, we are still children. We want to find a playmate for our thoughts and feelings.

Wilhelm Stekhel (1868–1940)
Austrian psychiatrist

There is no
hope of joy
except in human
relations.

ANTOINE DE SAINT-EXUPÉRY (1900–1944)
FRENCH AVIATOR AND WRITER

Friendship is so nearly allied to happiness, that one can hardly exist without the other.

Anonymous

Friendship with oneself is all-important, because without it one cannot be friends with anyone else in the world.

Eleanor Roosevelt (1884–1962)
American writer, lecturer, and First Lady

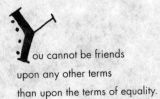

You cannot be friends
upon any other terms
than upon the terms of equality.

WOODROW WILSON (1856–1924)
28TH PRESIDENT OF THE UNITED STATES

Friendship is a strong and habitual inclination in two
persons to promote the good and happiness of one another.

Eustace Budgell (1686–1737)
English writer

. . . the responsibilities of friendship? . . . To talk. And to listen.

Rosie Thomas, b. 1947
English writer

That is a choice friend who conceals our
faults from the view of others. . .

WILLIAM SECKER
17TH-CENTURY ENGLISH CLERGYMAN

After all, it is not strength but weakness that endears. You don't make friends by being right all the time.

Havilah Babcock (1898–1964)
American professor and writer

*The growth
of true friendship
may be
a lifelong affair.*

Sarah Orne Jewett (1849–1909)
American writer

The reward of friendship is itself. The man who hopes for anything else does not understand what true friendship is.

AILRED [AETHELRED] OF RIEVAULX (C. 1110–1167)
ENGLISH HISTORIAN AND ABBOT

I think there is nothing
in the world so precious as truly
selfless friendship. . . .

Laurence Olivier (1907–1989)
English actor and writer

A friend is a person with whom you dare to be yourself.

Frank Crane (1861–1928)
American clergyman and writer

I always felt that the great high privilege, relief and comfort of friendship was that one had to explain nothing.

KATHERINE MANSFIELD (1888–1923)
ENGLISH WRITER

Forget your woes

when you see

your friend.

Priscian
6th-century Latin grammarian

We do not so much need the help of our friends as the confidence of their help in need.

Epicurus (341–270 B.C.)
Greek philosopher

Friendship consists in forgetting what one gives,
and remembering what one receives.

ALEXANDRE DUMAS (1802–1870)
FRENCH NOVELIST AND PLAYWRIGHT

If you're a person's friend, you
don't harp on things you know are
past their ever changing.

Allan Gurganus, b. 1947
American writer

Your friend is the man who knows all about you, and still likes you.

Elbert Hubbard (1856–1915)
American writer and editor

We cherish our friends not for their ability to amuse us, but for ours to amuse them.

EVELYN WAUGH (1903–1966)
ENGLISH WRITER

It's the friends
you can call
up at 4 A.M.
that matter.

Marlene Dietrich (1901–1992)
German-born American actress and singer

*What's friendship's realest measure? . . . The amount of precious time
you'll squander on someone else's calamities. . . .*

Richard Ford, b. 1944
American writer

When a friend asks
there is no tomorrow.

GEORGE HERBERT (1593–1633)
ENGLISH CLERGYMAN AND POET

Hold a true friend with both your hands.

What a luxury it was to spend time with old friends with whom it was okay to talk about nothing much.

Lisa Alther, b. 1944
American writer

. . . we have been talking as old
friends should talk, about nothing,
about everything.

LILLIAN HELLMAN (1906–1984)
AMERICAN PLAYWRIGHT

Sooner or later you've heard all your best friends have to say.

Then comes the tolerance of real love.

Ned Rorem, b. 1923
American composer and writer

. . . silence is not an embarrassment

between friends. . . .

David Niven (1909–1983)
English actor and writer

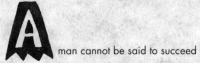

A man cannot be said to succeed
in this life who does not satisfy
one friend.

HENRY DAVID THOREAU (1817–1862)
AMERICAN NATURALIST AND WRITER